Pebble Plus

Pet Questions and Answers

PET BIRDS

Questions and Answers

by Christina Mia Gardeski

raintree

a Capstone company — publishers for children

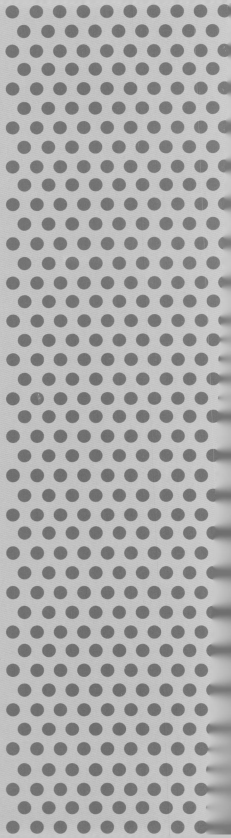

Raintree is an imprint of Capstone Global Library Limited, a company incorporated in England and Wales having its registered office at 264 Banbury Road, Oxford, OX2 7DY – Registered company number: 6695582

www.raintree.co.uk
myorders@raintree.co.uk

Edited by Carrie Braulick Sheely and Alesha Halvorson
Designed by Kayla Rossow
Picture research by Pam Mitsakos
Production by Gene Bentdahl

ISBN 978 1 4747 2141 7
20 19 18 17 16
10 9 8 7 6 5 4 3 2 1

British Library Cataloguing in Publication Data
A full catalogue record for this book is available from the British Library.

Acknowledgements

Alamy: Ashley Cooper, 4-5, Elena Abduramanova, 15, Eudyptula, 13, kungverylucky, 7, Tracy Starr, 11, Ulyana Vyugina, 19, VladisChern, 1, 22, Yuangeng Zhang, cover, zhuda, 21, Zurijeta, 17;
Thinkstock: einegraphic, 9, moodboard, 10

Printed and bound in China.

Contents

Who wants a bath?

My bird!

Birds love to stay clean.

They splash in bird baths.

Birds preen their feathers

with their beaks.

Do birds have ears?

Birds' ears are hard to see.

They are hidden by feathers.

Birds have one big ear hole

behind each eye. Most birds

can hear very well.

Why do birds sing?

Birds sing to talk to other birds. They sing to tell where they live and to show off. Many birds sing early in the morning.

Can my bird make me sneeze?

Birds shed their feathers and grow new ones. This is called moulting. Tiny bits of feather called dander can make you sneeze.

What do birds eat?

Pet birds eat pellets of bird food. They also like fresh fruit and vegetables. Keep their bowls away from droppings.

Give them clean water every day.

Where can I keep my bird?

Pet birds can live indoors in a big cage. Line it with clean paper. Put perches high and low in the cage. Add swings, ladders and bells for play.

Can I train my bird?

Birds are clever. Some birds can be trained to rest on your finger and do simple tricks.
Other birds can learn to talk.

Can I let my bird out of its cage?

It is healthy for a bird to spend time outside of its cage. But birds can get hurt flying indoors. Make a safe bird playroom. Hide cables. Close all windows and doors.

Does my bird need a friend?

Birds need friends just like you do!

Talk and play with your bird every day.

Let it hop on your hand. Get another

pet bird if you can.

Glossary

dander tiny bits of feathers or skin

droppings bird waste

moult to lose feathers regularly

pellet small, dry, rounded piece of bird food

perch rod on which a bird rests

preen make feathers neat and clean using the beak

shed fall or drop off

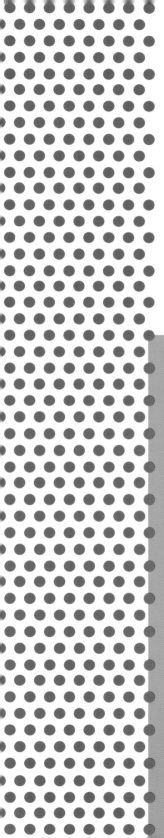

Read more

Beaky's Guide to Caring for your Bird (Pets' Guides),
Isabel Thomas (Raintree, 2015)

Birds (Animal Classification), Angela Royston (Raintree, 2015)

RSPB First Book of Birds, Anita Ganeri and David Chandler
(A&C Black Publishers, 2011)

Websites

www.bbc.co.uk/nature/life/Bird/by/rank/all

Learn about many types of bird, where birds live and what
they eat.

www.rspb.org.uk/discoverandenjoynature/families/children

Enjoy games and activities and learn more about wild birds.

Comprehension questions

1. What can you do to make it safe for your pet bird to fly indoors?

2. Do you think birds are good family pets?

Index